# OLD
# SOLDIERS
# NEVER DIE

# OLD SOLDIERS NEVER DIE

## The Legacy of W.A. Evans

MARLENE R. EVANS-ASKEW

ARPress
ILLUMINATING IDEAS,
EMPOWERING VOICES

**ARPress**
45 Dan Road Suite 5
Canton MA 02021
Hotline:        1(888) 821-0229
Fax:            1(508) 545-7580

Ordering Information:
Quantity sales.Special discounts are available on quantity purchases by corporations, associations, and others.For details, contact the publisher at the address above.

Printed in the United States of America.

ISBN-13:        Paperback        979-8-89330-105-2
                eBook            979-8-89330-106-9

Library of Congress Control Number: 2024900547

# DEDICATION

A Special Thanks To my Family, my loving children, Thereah, Octavia, Yolanda, Melvin and Patrick, who shared with me in this adventure, I also Share my memories with other family members and friends who so faithfully helped me as well in telling my story of growing up in a God Fearing Family.

# CONTENTS

# INTRODUCTION

Rev. Wallace A. Evans is my grandfather who lived to be 100 years old. He was born August 22, 1884 and he died November 29, 1984. My grandfather was a man among men. I have come to realize he will live on in all of us. If I were to sum up his life in a song it would be, ***"I'm A Soldier in the Army of The Lord."*** It is an honor to be labeled a soldier in the Lord's army. It's an even greater honor if your journey lasts 100 years.

His dedicated life has left a profound impartation upon mine. It has been a great pleasure and honor to write about him. Old soldiers, they don't die, they just fade away is both a poetic and prophetic way to sum up my grandfather's inspiring life.

# CHAPTER ONE

# IN THE BEGINNING

## The Early Years

Wallace Evans was born August 22, 1884 in Orangeburg, S.C. He was born to the union of Brantley and Lucy Evans. He was one of nine children – five boys and four girls.

His father was born in 1855. His mother was born in 1843.

His brothers:
Lawrence born 1880
Virgil born 1882
Isaiah, around 1883
Gary born 1895
His sisters:
Carrie born 1887
Flossie born 1891
Lottie born 1897
Louise born 1898

Wallace Evans worked in the field approximately nine months out of the year. But he was able to come into town and attend school at least 3 months out of the year. He was not able to finish his education; however, he learned to read and write very well. When he was around thirteen, he dropped out of school to work full-time to help his parents and the other siblings. His dream was to become a doctor.

He educated himself through reading and studying on his own. Education was important to him and he instilled that in us as well. Although, he never was able to fulfill his dream of becoming a medical doctor, down through the years he did become a doctor of the soul. Many came to know Christ under his ministry.

## 1920

In 1920 during the industrial revolution at the age of 35, he left Orangeburg, S.C. and traveled with his wife Hattie Evans who was 27 and daughter Lillie Evans who was 12 years old. Lillie lived through the early 30s but would pass before I was born in childbirth. The loss of Lillie and her child was a big blow to my grandmother and their deaths would be one of the reasons I would come to be raised by my grandparents. But that part of the story is for a little later.

When my grandparents first came to Florida, they settled in Palatka in Putnam County. Granddaddy landed a job of chipping boxes which was the work of the day. It was hard work. But it was honest work and it afforded him the opportunity to take care of his family.

## Englewood

This is a picture of Englewood, Florida over a 100 years ago. It still looked just like this in the early forties when I was young. It was as if our town had been preserved in time. Not far from where we lived there were even artifacts found at the Indian Mound Park area that dated as far back as 400 B.C. Historians believe that this area had once been inhabited by the Calusa Indians.

However, before my grandfather would migrate to Florida, his early years were spent in South Carolina. He was 12 years old living in Orangeburg, South Carolina when the town of Englewood, Florida was established. Little did he know, that the town he would end up spending more than ½ his life, was being established.

In 1896, Herbert Nicholas, Englewood III and his two brothers came to this area with the hopes of building a business by growing lemons. It had been discovered that vitamin C would cure scurvy. As a result, there was a high demand for citrus goods.

This endeavor promised to be very profitable for the brothers. But the mammoth freezes in 1894 and 1895 brought disaster and destruction to the lemon trees from Tampa to Fort Myers. Killing that part of their dream. And, although there was never again a freeze compared to this one, promoters had lost faith in the area as a market for large scale secure citrus development and the brothers knew they had to change their tactics to lure investors.

So, the brothers took lemons and turned them into lemonade. They began to promote that part of the Lemon Bay area as a great place for raising families, to retire and to live a laid-back lifestyle of fishing and hunting. In 1897 the area, which is now known as Lemon Bay, had a population of 86 people. This area included Grove City and adjoining areas. Land was selling for $30 an acre in 1910. Today, Englewood's population is close to 80,000.

For any town or city to thrive it was important that there be some type of industry or business that could economically support the families that were moving in. The lumber industry was also booming in the United States and the Englewood's area was ripe to take advantage of this booming industry trade. The Englewood area continued to grow.

In 1923 railroad tires, booming construction and turpentine production produced jobs. My grandfather would come to this area in later years following the work trail moving from the St. Augustine and Palatka areas and found work and settled in the Englewood area.

My grandfather had a nose and head for business and followed the migration pattern caused by the industrial revolution. From the beginning, Britain's colonies in North America were encouraged to produce pine tar and pitch, and to collect gum from pine trees for later shipment to England and the Carolinas encouraged by the Bounty Act of 1705.

At that time, England had been cut off from its Scandinavian supplies by Russia's invasion of Sweden-Finland. By 1725 four fifths of the tar and pitch used in England came from the American colonies.

The American Revolution in 1776 would cause England to again trade with the Dutch for Scandinavian products. As the population of the United States grew and moved west, forests were cleared. By 1850 most of the U.S. production of tar and pitch was in North and South Carolina. As the 19th Century progressed, tar, pitch and turpentine manufacturing spread south and west into the state of Georgia, Alabama, Mississippi, Louisiana, Texas, and Florida. By 1900, rosin and turpentine were the dominant products, and the states of Georgia, Florida, and Alabama were the three major producers.

Granddaddy had left his home, in Orangeburg, South Carolina to follow the job opportunities. His first stop in Florida was in the St. Augustine and Palatka areas. However, he would not settle there. His travels finally landed him in the Englewood area where he would make his home for over 70 years.

<u>Life Before Electricity 1940—1951</u> Kerosene lamps and outdoor toilets 1941 was the year World War II broke out, Franklin D. Roosevelt was elected President of the US for a third term and Winston Churchill was appointed Prime Minister of England. It was also one year after I was born. Back then the main group who did the migrant farm work were Blacks. My mother

was part of this generation. She would leave us in the care of my Grandfather and Grandmother as she travelled around the country following the harvesting schedule.

I would be the first of Wallace A. Evans grandchildren or (Granddaddy as every subsequent generation would call him) to come live with them when I was seven months old. Over a period of 4 years, there would be two other grandchildren added to our family, Willis Evans Jr. and Loreine Evans- Townsel. Would all be raised by our grandparents on our father's side.

Over the years our other little sister, Chloe would also come to spend time with us out at Granddaddy's place from time to time. Daddy as we called him; also, was never a stranger to hard work. So, to him it was no big deal to take on the responsibility of raising a second batch of children in his late 50s

When I look back over that time in my life, I am reminded of some of my first memories. They all seem to be centered on my Grandfather, Wallace A. Evans. I sometimes shake my head because I now live in a world where TV is not only in color, but I can watch it on my phone. It is a lot different than what life was like when I was a kid. Life was different then. Not necessarily bad just different. For example, how many people woke up this morning in America gave any serious thought about running water. In the 1940s, when I was a little girl, we had no running water in our house. Our water came from a pump that was located at the left side of the house just beyond the bamboo trees.

It was like a scene from Little House on the Prairie. The outdoor toilet was erected behind the house to the far left about two hundred and fifty feet away from the house. Instead of plug-ins we had to use lime to deodorize the outhouse.

It's also hard to imagine life without electricity and so many other things we now take for granted. Back then, our home was not wired and at night we used kerosene lamps. Granddaddy would get the kerosene from the Filling Station at Cash's Corner or sometimes he would drive up to Mr. L. A. Anger's grocery store and buy it from Mr. Chuck's Gas Station which was nearby. These were your two options in the Forties in the Englewood area.

# CHAPTER TWO

# THE EARLY YEARS – THE 40S

A Time of War. A Man of Peace

It's hard to imagine at almost 2 years old having memories, but it is amazing what sticks in a person's mind. I remembered the Saturday of December 7, 1941. My grandfather was sitting near the radio in our living room with his hand resting on the 6x3 size battery radio, listening to the announcement that Pearl Harbor has just been bombed. And on that day, the war had begun for America.

The first round of Japanese bullets had hit Hawaii; Honolulu was now under attack. President Roosevelt's new challenging moment of leadership for the country was now being acted upon.

I remembered so well my grandfather grasping every piece of news he could get. He would read the Tampa Morning Tribune, which he read repeatedly most times, sometimes 3 times a day. During this tragic time, there was not much time for other radio activity. The Amos and Andy Show and many other listening entertainments were now skipped over.

As the war raged on, Granddaddy would faithfully drive the four miles every day to Cash's Corner or L.A. Anger's Grocery store to purchase a paper and get any other reading material that was available the "first thing" in the morning. We had two grocery stores in the Englewood area. The other store was Tate's Groceries.

*Englewood Sun*
PHOTO COURTESY OF DIANA HARRIS

*Englewood Sun*
PHOTO COURTESY OF DIANA HARRIS

*Englewood Sun*
PHOTO COURTESY OF DIANA HARRIS

*(My Uncle Paul Herring worked at this Beach House)*

And the Post Office, I remembered so well, Granddaddy taking us to this place. Stamps were one cent per post card and five for a regular stamp.

For so many people in America, the war had become personal. I remember my father (Willis Evans) going off to war in 1943. After his basic training, he was shipped off to France. My father was an auto mechanic, and his skills became even more sharpened because of his assignment in the U.S. Army.

*Down the Street*
Photo Courtesy of Down the Street by Sonja Thomas Wright

My grandfather and grandmother Hattie, were left with the three of us to raise. Loreine, the youngest, Willis Jr. and I who was the oldest. There was never a dull moment with war in action and all the chores at home. The church work and keeping bread on the table and tending after a wife and three grandchildren kept him very busy.

While the war was raging overseas, many changes were taking place at home. Nevertheless, there were still some things that pretty much stayed the same. My early years included a time when the cattle would roam all over the roads. Most people when they hear talk about roaming cattle, they think Texas, or Montana but Florida in certain parts had its share as well. The cattle ran in herds sometimes from one side of the open fields to another - and up and across the road.

Many accidents were caused as a result of cattle crossing the road when, at the same time a car would be coming down the road. It was especially dangerous at night. There were bends you had to look out for when you were coming around a curb between San Castle and McCall and again, between El Jobean and Murdock. The roads were not lit.

I remembered one night on our way back from church service, my grandfather didn't hit his brakes in time and this brimmed bull charged right into the car. The car almost turned around and over on the road that night. Thank God, the only damage that was done was that one light beam was knocked out.

What a miracle! We were spared that night from a more serious accident that would be just one of the many miracles we would see in our family. I genuinely believe because of how faithful my grandfather was over taking caring the Lord's folks that night God took care of his. The Lord had his angels on assignment looking over us. Grandaddy was a real man of faith and it was one of the things he tried to instill in all of us.

**LOREINE**

This wasn't the only miracle we experienced in our family. Miracles was a way of life for us from as early as I can remember. There was this one time when we were very small and my sister Loreine became sick unto death. She was about two years old and her temperature was so high, she began to have convulsions. Her eyes were glazed over, while she lay staring at the ceiling. She was speechless, and she started foaming at the mouth, and then my grandmother began screaming.

My grandfather said to her, "get out of the room old lady" and he fell on his knees beside the bed, snatched off her flannel gown

11

and asked for a bottle of vinegar. He poured the vinegar over her naked body. He began to cry out to the Lord. My sister lifeless body began to cool, and she began to move. Her life was restored.

I witnessed my grandfather carry out the same act that Peter had done in the Bible in Acts 9:36-43 verses. Peter raised Tabitha from the dead. 37th verse;

*"And it came to pass in those days, that she was sick, and died, who when they had washed, they laid her in an upper chamber."*

*They sent for Peter. 39th verse: Then Peter arose and went with them when he was come, they brought him to the upper chamber; 40th verse: But Peter put them all forth and kneeled (He put them out of the room) Kneeling down praying, and turning himself to the body and said, "Tabitha, arise" and she opened her eyes and when she saw Peter, she sat up. And he gave her his hand and lifted her up."*

My grandfather didn't just preach the word. He lived the word. He believed that Jesus Christ was the same yesterday, today and forever more. So, he knew that if God had given Peter the power through the Holy Ghost to raise the dead, then he too had the faith to believe that, that same power could work through him. Peter demonstrated this power; I was a witness to my sister, Loreine, being the recipient of that same power operating through my grandfather.

He refused to give up on any of us. He faced every challenge with faith and will power. My sister Loreine would be the first one in our family to attend college. She would later become a teacher and help thousands of children in the Miami area receive their education. She would teach for over 25 years in the public-school system. I can't tell you how many lives were touched in a positive way because my grandfather refused to let her die all those years ago.

### The Acts of the Forties continued:

Yes, the war was on, but provision was at home. We picked guavas and blueberries in their seasons. Guava jelly, guava doopy and guava pies were specials. We picked the fruit; granddaddy and grandmother processed them for jarring; for when she would make pies. A guava pie was so good. She would put a little lemon extract in her pies, as well. Baking took place year-round. Another special dish was chicken feet, sometimes cooked in rice. Loreine loved this dish. She still makes this dish to this day.

One of the special dishes my grandmother would make was sweet potato pies. Her favorite spices were nutmeg and cinnamon. Nutmeg would always be in her T-Cakes she would bake. Granddaddy made sure that we had the best stove. I remember the range with the double decker tickets on top. A place your baked goods were placed. He was in the wood business, and he made sure we had enough fat wood for baking and cooking.

Another one of my grandmother's favorite dishes was Highland Turtle Soup. The common name for this turtle was gopher. We spent many days in the woods with my grandfather digging gophers for her. He just loved making her happy. The recipe for making turtle soup: onions, garlic at times, green peppers, salt and pepper. The brown gravy made from scratch. Yes, all steamed down and a pot of dry white rice. We even had it for breakfast sometimes, served over grits.

We grew up in the sticks as they called it. But, to us it was just being raised in the country. Oh yes, my grandfather knew how to provide.

# CHAPTER THREE

# GROWING UP IN THE 40S & 50S WHAT A LIFE!

There was plenty of work during the early forties. The war was on and there was a great need for tar and charcoal. Grandaddy was not only a pastor, but he was an entrepreneur. He was highly respected by both whites and blacks in our community.

**The Making and Burning of a Tar Kiln:**

Granddaddy oversaw the entire project and would hire his own crew. Many of the men came from Punta Gorda and Murdock. There was one other contractor that worked along with my grandfather. He too was a black man who came from Punta Gorda. He was Mr. John Whaley. He traveled the twenty-three miles from Punta Gorda to the Kiln site. He also brought along his own crew. These two men played a big role in providing employment for many of the local black men. There were many nights when he would stay up all night watching the tar being run. Looking back years later, I can see that my grandfather and Mr. John Whaley assisted in making A.C. Frizzell a millionaire. Granddaddy was a very hard worker and he, unfortunately, was paid a lot less than what he was worth to do this work. But despite all of this, we never went hungry, we never went unclothed, and we were never cold.

*A.C. Frizzell*
http://ccflhistory.contentdm.oclc.org/cdm/ref/collection/
p15007coll1/id/7940

Pine Tar Production and the production of charcoal were star products of my grandfather's contractual agreements. This was one of the most interesting things I observed during this industrial age. The project of the production of tar was a very detailed endeavor. The work put in to producing drums of pine tar was done in a very strategic way. The fat wood is stacked in a saucer shape concrete pit that holds up to twenty cords of wood with a vat outlet. My grandfather and his crew were highly skilled, and they took pride in themselves in producing only the highest quality of pine tar. It took approximately three to four weeks to construct a kiln. There was a lot of work that went into this including finding the best fatwood. This meant selecting the nice tall pine trees, cutting them down and cutting them up and making the pieces into about twenty-four to thirty – two inches of split pieces, hauled from the various parts of the woods and stacked into the round concrete vat that holds fifteen to twenty truckloads of wood.

The creation of tar was not a process that you could rush. You had to know when not to expose the burning fat wood to, too much air. When the winds shifted sometimes at night, special techniques had to be administered to slow down the flames. This was done to enable a good flow of tar to run freely from the center of the concrete pit through the pipeline to the vat. After the adjustment of the flames, the steady flow of tar would run sometimes for most of the night. The art of adjusting the flames were simply shoveling shovels of sand from one area of the kiln and throwing them on the area where the flames were burning to fast as a result getting to much wind from the shifting of the wind. Once the flames were under control and the tar was flowing, the dippers would take turns each using what was a size two bucket with a long handle. These tar dippers uniforms consisted of high-top shoes, socks and long sleeve jumper jeans. They were better called overhauls and a jumper jacket. They took their safety measures very seriously, however, despite all of this, the men would still end up looking like gigantic tar babies and they smelled like pine tar as well. It would take almost a week or more before these men would go back to smelling like a normal person.

The tar that was produced was poured into a hundred-gallon drum. For each drum, my grandfather was paid approximately $100. $5,000.00 was a good amount to be made during this era. Each kiln produced approximately fifty or more drums of tar which was shipped overseas and various parts of the United States. There were three (hundred-gallon drums) placed on a truck and taken to the nearby railroad station which was nine miles down the road from the burning site. The shipping station was located at McCall. This was the route coming from Boca Grande, Fla. that connected so many other towns in Florida.

Most of the kilns that were burned by my grandfather were done about ¾ of a mile away from the house. Mr. Jessie was there, as well, as his brother Mr. John Mitchell. who lived right down the road from the location of the kiln site. We were truly blessed because we had neighbors who would volunteer to help us get the work done and that was such a plus.

No one in my family was exempted from the process. My brother, Willis Jr., sister, Loreine and myself had to stay out there, as well! We wrapped up in blankets and rubbed six- twelve on us and slept on the ground at night right along with my grandfather. He included us in all his work experiences. Human resources, natural resources, your name it, we were all a part of that industrial era as well.

After the kiln was burned, the charcoal was gathered and piled in a field right behind our house and then sold. A bushel was sold for five dollars and a half -of- bushel went for three dollars. Many years later, charcoal went up to seven dollars for a half bushel. Business was good all year round, especially during the winter months.

Coals were used for a variety of things; such as barbecuing and for water purification. There were even times when my grandfather was away, that I would oversee the coal sales. The customers would come from a long distance just to buy the coals. People would travel from the Lemon Bay area, Englewood, Grove City and Placida.

When my grandmother's health began to fail her, Daddy did almost everything. He drove the school bus from the early fifties until about the middle fifties. He would bus us from Englewood to Punta Gorda to connect with the school bus to Fort Myers for high school. He also made sure that there was food for us to eat, all cooked and prepared for us when we return from school in the evening.

I remember one time he had made a pot of string beans, white potatoes and fresh pork neck bones together and in doing so, he had cooked onion peelings as well in the pot of food. I sometimes would speak out about his cooking and got rebuked. He labeled me as being so observant and talkative. Another time, granddaddy had cooked her a hamburger and the ground meat was labeled cat food and I told my grandmother what the label said. She never ate another hamburger. Oh well, I just talked too much. Days, yes, back in the day!

*Our Times in The Days of Rev. Wallace Evans*

Our home was always open, that's just who Granddaddy and Grandmother were. One example of his kindness is shared by our cousin Mary (Herring) Upshur:

I remember there were days when Hattie Evans looked after us for our mother Darkus Herring. She would travel back and forth between Safety Harbor and Englewood, Florida. We would stay with Reverend Evans for days sometimes weeks at a time. I remembered one Sunday morning we were getting ready for church we dressed the baby and sat her in a chair near the door.

The rest of us went off to finish dressing and headed for the car. We had driven close to 15 miles before any of us realized that we had left the baby at the house and had to drive about 15 miles back to go get her. When Rev. Evans got back to the house, she was still sitting in a chair on the porch, where we had placed her.

Rev. Evans opened his home to everybody. We had many good times staying with them. I remember another time we went into the pasture to pick some oranges and grapefruits. Although we were told not to go in the pasture on more than one occasion, we were typical children, and as soon as Rev. Evans was not looking, we went anyway.

We would, folks would call, hard-headed and even though we knew there were bulls in the field where the fruit was, we went any way. We picked our fruit and were leaving, when we saw the cows coming toward us, we had to run and climbed up the nearest tree. The cows circled the tree and would not leave until feeding time. Boy! We were afraid. No one came to look for us until late in the afternoon. We knew that we were in trouble. We started home and met someone coming to look for us. That was just one of the many days in the life with the Rev. Evans and family.

There were many good days and some bad days that were shared with these loving and caring God- fearing people. I will never forget those days. They helped make me what I am today. The importance of Holiness is one of the things that stayed in my mind all these years. Those memories will never leave. I accepted Christ one day as a child. He helped to jump start us on the right road.

*The Cousins **Mary, Verna, Loreine, Paul, Stack, Marlene, Lisa, Erlean***

There are places we go; people we meet on this life's journey that set the course for our lives. When I look back over my life I can honestly say, thank God that Reverend Evans played such an important part in our lives.

## With love always, Cousin Mary

*Cousin Mary and her children*

*The Cousins*

## The Storms Life

Storms were not unusual when you live near the Gulf. I remember hurricane season. Believe me the fear of God and the presence of God were the two dominating factors in my grandfather's legacy. The announcement of a tropical storm or hurricane was the instrument in which he used to exemplify his faith in God.

In 1945 a major storm had a direct hit on southern Florida. This storm had winds gusts as high as 170 mph. And impacted from Miami all the way to our area of Florida.

This storm that hit Englewood was really devastating in many ways. My grandfather did the routine thing. He gathered sheets of tin and nailed up the windows all around the house. We'd pray and following his leading, we were all grouped in the living room. There was Granddaddy listening to the battery radio absorbing every piece of news regarding the hurricane. We seemed to get the worst of the damage from the storms during the night. Usually by morning the worst would have blown over, but this time, the greatest hit came during the day. To see the forces of the wind and rain come in the daylight, is a fearful thing. We had a big chinaberry tree in the front yard that shaded most of the front yard.

This time, the power of the winds from the storm was so forceful, that it split this big tree in two. Seeing it split, uprooted and falling at the same time, left me trembling and almost speechless. One part of the fallen tree landed almost hitting the front porch. I knew only God saved us. It was the prayers that sustained us in such a desperate time.

It wouldn't be the only storm we would live through. At the home place, I remember another time in which there was an unusual lighting strike. A bolt of lightning came right over my head and struck down several cattle in a fenced in field which was about one-half mile ahead of me. There laid dead cattle stricken by lightning. I remembered rounding up the goats that had been grazing across the road in another field that was opposite of the house. Here is a little unknown fact, goats hate getting wet, which would explain why they smell the way they do. They seemed to have been as fearful as I was running toward the house.

The goats ran and would and hide right under the house. There were bill goats, nanny goats and baby goats (kids) as many as could get under the house, did so. The aftermath of the rain, wind and storm left such a bad smell from the wet goats that it would give you a headache. The fumes from the wet ground combined with the smelly goats were hard to get rid of. It was not until the sun came out and the fresh breeze start blowing again did, we get any relief.

Another time there was this one storm that came through bringing destruction right into our front yard. I saw the Chinaberry tree which stood less than 20 feet from our house split in half when the storm passed through our hometown. The memory still resonates so vividly. It was broad day when the winds escalated. The force of the wind was so powerful that it split the tree in half ...knocking half the tree down; while the other half of the tree remained standing. The part of the tree that fell, landed in our yard with a portion of it landing on our porch.

Yes, oh yes, I believe in the power of prayer saved us from a greater impact upon the house. Granddaddy, sitting right in the living room, doing what he did best, praying, while the storm ragged. Believe me, it's a fearful sight to see the acts of a storm in the daytime. But what is an even greater wonder to see how the power of prayer can protect you from and through the storm.

The power of the wind and the power of prayer. My little song because of this experience is. (Mark 4:38)

Careth not that we perish? My song, my answer: Yes, my Jesus cares.

I know it may feel like I have spent a great deal of time talking about storms but some of the greatest lessons I have learned has been the result of physical storms as well as spiritual storms My grandfather taught us that the storms are going to come but no matter what the storms look like, like the old man, you should never lose your faith.

## Church Life

God was always the center of my Grandfather Pastor Rev. W.A. Evan's life. His faith in God was what made him who he was and in turn helped make us who we are. Every Wednesday night we had a prayer meeting in our home in Englewood, Florida. We had wood floors with no carpeting.

I can remember how we had to scrub the floors with a brush using warm lye solution. At Grandaddy's house, everybody had an assignment. We had to make sure that the furniture was covered with a white sheet and the arms of the chair were covered with a white pillowcase. We washed the lamp shades and we put out the best shades for church service (the big white flowered designed shades). The lamp wicks had to be trimmed for the results of giving a much better flame.

Friday nights and Sunday Services:

Granddaddy conducted services in two locations. Beside the church services he held at home, the larger church was eighteen miles from

Englewood, off route 776. Of course, this was Murdock, and this was where the main church site was. It was also where the larger Black community was located. The people were very close knitted. We all knew each other. Some of the families that lived in the

Murdock community or the: The Murdock Quarters as it was called also from about 1945-1955 where:

1. Mr. Jerry & Mr. Gene
2. Mr. Bug & Mrs. Annie Lee
3. Mr. T. Model & Mrs. Naomi
4. Mr. Edgar & Mrs. Sarah Platt
5. Mr. George & Mrs. Bertha Buiey
6. Mr. Charlie & Mrs. Georgia Mae McNealy
7. Mr. Son & Mrs., Becky Smith
8. Mr. Sammie & Mrs. Hattie Kings
9. Mr. Buddie Price & Mrs. Annie Lou
10. Mr. J.C. Beauford Mr. Roscoe who lived across the railroad

Friday nights, Sunday and Sunday nights.

   Community church and fellowship was very important to my grandfather. Friday nights were rice night. On this night the members were responsible for bringing a pound of some form of food: rice, meal, flour, sugar, and can goods, of course, otherwise, you could always bring a dollar if you didn't have your pound of goods. Of course, this form of giving was to help support the pastor and his family. He had a wife and three grandchildren to be responsible for. There was no salary in those days; in this denomination, especially, the Movement we were in (The House of God Which Is the Church of The Living God the Pillar and Ground of The Truth…1Tim.3:15). My grandfather would have never survived from what the membership giving provided. He served the Lord because of the love he had for Him and His people. Granddaddy's service to the people was more than they could ever give back to him. I saw President J.F. Kennedy's philosophy lived out in him: "Ask not what your country can do for you, but what can you do for your country."

   First and third Sundays were pastoral days. Communion and feet washing were also administered at these times. The traditional doxology was never done on these nights. Instead, after feet washing, a hymn was always sung (one of the hymns stanzas was (Dark was the night and cold was the ground) and everyone would march out of the church and go their several ways upon returning to their homes. Some walked to the quarters where they lived, and others returned to their cars and traveled the distance they lived to reach their homes. My grandfather pastured at Murdock for over 30 years. Altogether, he had pastured for over fifty years. The last church that he presided as Pastor is still standing. The assistant pastor, Rev. Benjamin Brown is the grandson of a distant relative who used to be a member of Granddaddy's flock. Mae Francis Brown, was the mother of Benjamin Brown, who also served in a Pastoral position at the same location.

*Photos courtesy of Elizabeth Perkins*

## TRANSPORTATION

It was fall 1948, the time to attend the Assembly. The first time we as children were able to go along with Granddaddy. I remember so well; we traveled from Palmetto, Fl. to St. Petersburg by way of the ferry.

Of course, this was the only way to get to St. Pete. The old man has just bought another car. A station wagons this time a green Desoto. We had plenty of room for riding. We were able to stay right in the car as he drove right up on to that ferry and took that four-mile ride to St. Pete. What fun that was! What an experience! Loreine, Willis Jr. and myself along with our grandmother, Hattie Evans. We stayed from that Friday night until Sunday night. Which was the closing of the Assembly.

Reverend Evans, pastor of the Murdock, Fla. church. He was such an outstanding preacher, the Bishop would mostly, always choose my grandfather to be the pastor and speaker to preach the closing message. To list one of the most unique sermons: **Give Me a Man**. This one came from the book of Revelation, 5: 4&5 verses. My grandfather and his theological way of putting this sermon together, which was amazing. He told in detail how the earth had been searched to find someone worthy to go on man's bond to save a dying man. Man had sinned since Adam's day and need a redeemer, needed someone worthy to be that sacrifice.

But the great price was, it had to be a man found that had no sin found in his life. Many great men records were searched. The angels left heaven and came down to the lower world looking for a man to be that man. While the search was on, Abraham's record really stood out. Father of the faithful. But he couldn't be the man who was without blemish he told a lie when he went down in Egypt. He said Sarah was his sister instead of his wife. The angle searched Moses record, but Moses couldn't be the man, he slew an Egyptian while being on the back side of the mountain. Another great sermon was: Who is left among you that saw this house in her first glory and how do you see it now? Haggai.2:3. A special word to his descendants and to the other church folks. Personally, I feel he's looking down from glory asking the question, how are you carrying on in carrying out the works of the Lord?

## The Early Years – The 50s

### CHLOE

Every new decade always brings about change. My sister Chloe was born July 11th, 1950 in Punta Gorda, Florida. She would be the first black child born in at Charlotte County Hospital. Stack, Loreine and I had all been born with a midwife. Our Aunt Lillie had died over 20 years earlier in childbirth and even after all those years the trauma of it still impacted our family.

Ms. Mary (Chloe's Mom) was having a hard pregnancy and nobody wanted to take a chance. Our family had experienced first-hand what could happen to a woman who didn't have the right medical care if something went wrong during labor. So, they got permission for Ms. Mary to give birth in the "white only" hospital that was in Punta Gorda (Charlotte County) Fl. God showed us favor and Dr. Clemmons helped to bring her into the world. As a matter of fact, Chloe was given the middle name of Juanita after the white nurse that help to deliver her.

Looking back now, I can say how she was birthed, was a sign that would follow her, her entire life. For Chloe this wouldn't be the only *"first of"* that she would accomplish. She was always one to take the lead in making a mark or taking a stand when she thought something wasn't right.

I remember when she was about 4 or 5 years old, she had come out to stay with us in Englewood and something happened, and she couldn't get her way. She got an attitude. She went into the room, packed her little suitcase, went outside and stood on the front porch with her doll baby and with one shoe on; not being able to find the other shoe and told all of us she was going home. By way of hiking to Fort Myers, Fl; which was 50 miles away. She was going back to her other grandmother. Her mother's mother. I believe that is when Granddaddy started calling her "Sweet

Thing". I believe he was trying to call those things that weren't into existence.

I don't believe he was trying to kill her spirit or make her into something she was not, but he knew that it was important that that fiery spirit and energy needed to be challenged into a positive force.

She would later be one of the first black children to integrate the public schools in Hillsborough County. She along with 5 other black children would attend West Tampa Junior High School in the early Sixties. She would win Miss Freshman in 1968. At FAMU in Tallahassee, Florida where she attended.

Just like our grandfather, she has spent her life and career fighting to make a positive impact for those in her community. She has not won every battle, but she continues to fight. And that is because the old soldier didn't just raise grandchildren, he raised soldiers to continue to fight the good fight even after he was gone.

US Rep. Kathy Castor, US Rep. John Lewis & Chloe Coney

Chloe Evans-Coney is the 5th grandchild of Rev. W.A. Evans. If I were to share a now word to describe how this seed has blossomed, I would say...

*...and his seed shall be blessed.*

*His seed shall be mighty in the land. The generation of the upright will be blessed. (Psalm 112:2 (KJV)*

*His offspring will be mighty in the land; the generation of the upright will be blessed.*

*The English Standard Version (ESV)*

*His offspring will be mighty in the land; the generation of the upright will be blessed.*

*Psalm. 102:28*

*The children of your servants will dwell securely, and their descendants will be established before you.*

*Yes, old soldier, you didn't die, you just faded away.*

## THEN THERE WAS LIGHT

The early fifties gave birth to other experiences such as us having electricity. The Vanderbilt Brothers, William and Fred brought up the areas of the pastureland between San Castle and McCall (Route 776) two thirds of the land was used for racehorse breeding and most of the other portion of the land was used for a guava grove.

For this reason, electricity was extended from the township of Lemon Bay and Englewood to McCall. Our home site was located right between these points of the electricity extension. 1952 was a new beginning, the lamps and shades were out, and the bulbs and lights were in.

Despite the addition of electricity, we were not completely modern; we still had the outdoor toilet and the water pump that was approximately two feet from the cluster of bamboo trees that was to the left side of our house.

### How He Utilized His Skills

My grandfather was a very hard-working man and he was an entrepreneur. He always had more than one iron in the fire. As a result, we grew up having multiple sources of income.

He secured the job of putting fence up from San Castle to McCall. The fence extended fourteen or more miles. Once the first phase of the task was completed my grandfather was hired to work on another contracting job. He along with his hired labor, took months to get this job done. The finding and cutting of the posts which took truck loads and truckloads of pine trees cut and manicured in post length for the job. Believe me, it was work for the entire summer and most of the fall of that year. Once the post holes were dug and the posts placed securely, the unrolling and setting of the barb wire was the second phase of the task.

The fenced in area from just beyond our house beginning from the wild oak and orange grove was the area for the racehorse. This area was called the 2-V Ranch (Vanderbilt Brothers) of course their winter or seasonal homes were down on Manasota

Beach. This is mostly where all the wealthy and rich white people lived.

Our house sat right off Route 776 on the McCall Road and was surrounded with natural resources. We were just blessed by the forces of nature. There was a rock pit just a mile and a half to the right of us. In the summer months my grandfather and his crew busted rock and hauled them. They were sold for yard decoration and boat basin work. Every waterfront home had a boat basin. Most of the homes were done with the finished work of the big white rocks. The creativity of the yards at these homes were amazing. They were also filled with beautiful tropical plants and flowers.

## The Land

*A Rock Pit*

I also remembered well the first $5 my brother Stack made. He helped with the planting of the guava trees. He dug the holes to place the guava plants in the ground. He was paid this nice crisp five-dollar bill for his work. Just think an eleven-year-old boy, in the 50s having earned a nice new bill of money. He saved that money. Really, I don't know how long.

When the winter season, came every home had a fireplace, therefore, the business was firewood. My grandfather furnished many of the homes on the beach and many others in the Lemon Bay area, Englewood and Manasota Keys with firewood.

I was instrumental in helping him cut and stack many coils of wood. I even helped him to deliver the firewood. Half coils were often sold as well. Self- employed, entrepreneur, you name it, that's what my grandfather was.

## The Livestock

Among the livestock, there was a horse, mule, a small herd of cattle, (oh course for milk), chickens, eggs, many hogs and many goats. We had so many goats at one time, folks started calling our living area Goatsville. The story about the hogs and goats is really mind blowing. The cows had to be branded as well as the hogs. They wandered in herds or groups. They graze and lived mostly in the pastures further away from our home. They lived off wild berries, palmetto berries for sure...grass and the wild fruit that grew. They wandered away in the woods and stayed some time weeks and months.

They sometimes mixed with others stock. So, it was very important to have your stocked branded. We were on the hips of the aged stock. Oh course, this stood for Wallace Evans. Many of the hogs were sold on the market for income benefit. Cattles as well.

When processing hogs for market, the stock was put in a fenced in area, then fed food with a soap- mixture ingredient; the soap was made of lye. This would purify them for market sales. This would kill the parasites in hogs that would be sold. I learned how to clean chitterlings. I learned how to make hog head cheese back in the day. What an exciting time!

## The Water

My grandfather's house was surrounded with patches of blueberries, blackberries, huckleberries, guavas, oranges and grapefruits; there were lots of means for us to live off the land. But we were also exposed to plenty of seafood. For us there were even more: fish, all sorts of fish, clams, crabs etc.

Our uncle, my grandfather's brother-in-law was a fisherman that lived six miles away right down on the beach. The beach that was adjacent to Lemon Bay that emptied into the Gulf of Mexico. Our uncle fished for a living. We were so blessed to get all the surplus fish that was not sold on the market, many times we were able to obtain tubs of fish. To this day my family loves some seafood. It is all our all-time favorite meal.

Blessed of the Lord and highly favored was a true echo. Yes, and I say so!

## ... and The Good Times Just Rolled On

I observed my grandfather's style of raising his grandchildren. In my opinion, he demonstrated a very balanced approach in his style. although we grew up in a country location. He would take us to town (Punta Gorda, Fla.) after leaving church on most Friday nights. Murdock was the location of the church site, which was eight miles away from Punta Gorda, going to town is where we had our social moments. We would go to the movies that cost 25 cents. We would see the good old Westerns like Hopalong Cassidy, The Lone Ranger, Roy Rogers, Dale Evans and Gene Autry. My grandfather was very religious, but he believed in a balanced life for his grandchildren.

## THEN THERE WAS THE HOLIDAYS

Thanksgiving was observed normally at home. Since we lived a distance from the church, we just cooked and stayed at home with the family. Of course, my grandmother made those sweet potato pies, tea cakes, lemon pies and all the fresh fruits were also among our dinner group of foods. Our turkey was never too big of a bird for some reason.

Christmas was the most exciting time. We were blessed with so many gifts and many baskets of fruit. Some of the gifts were clothing: coats, dresses, sweaters, and shoes.

My sister Loreine reminded me of the times we received what would be the equivalent of a gift card from the Vanderbilt's, they had a store in Englewood and that is how we got our shoes. They also gave us a silver dollar piece. Grandma wouldn't let us spend it but made us put it up and save it. We were so excited for Christmas, so much, that we could not barely contain ourselves.

The Vanderbilt's, the Rockefeller's and A.C. Frizzell (the millionaire that owned Murdock and most of El Jobean) were some of the very wealthy people that lived on the beach. These were also the ones that made this season the greatest for us.

### STACK AKA Willis Evans Jr.

We had a good life but like in all things, there were moments that came that would try our faith. We had to travel from Englewood to Murdock for the Sunday afternoon and evening services. This afternoon, I remembered so very well how my brother Willis Jr. (Stack) had gotten dressed early and he had gone outside to gather some objects to throw at the people that would be standing on the El Jobean bridge fishing.

He had collected some old rotten onions and tomatoes to use for throwing at the people. Once you threw the objects, you would have to duck, lay down and cover up your head underneath the piece of canvas. Willis Jr. reached into the bag and comes out with an overripe tomato, winds up his left arm, aim, and throws hitting a white lady right in her face. The smashed tomato not only covered half her face but ran down spotting up her blouse as well. Little did we know that the woman's husband had seen everything that had happened. There is an expression that God looks after babies and fools. We were our grandfather's babies, but that day Stack was playing the role of a fool.

These people immediately got into their car and began to follow us. By the time we had reached Murdock, which was another eight miles down the road my grandfather began to slow down to make the turn off the highway, when suddenly the car that had trailed us from El Jobean, pulled up beside the truck and began to beckon to him.

I remember the white man saying to Granddaddy, *"I have something to say to you. One of those children that's riding in the back of your truck threw a rotten tomato and hit my wife in the face while we were fishing on the bridge. I am calling the police on your children."*

My grandfather, somehow, managed to convince this very angry white man that he would handle the matter. The man was persuaded to just leave my brother in his hands. For us it was just an innocent prank. What we didn't fully grasp was the danger he had put the entire family in. In the early 40s there was no Black Live Matters movement.

Desegregation had not happened, and racism was not overt. If you were white you didn't get fired from your job for calling someone a nigger or wearing a black face. Something like this could have gotten our entire family killed. We were not born yet, but my Grandfather lived through the time of the Rosewood massacre in 1923. As a matter of fact, we had family who ended up migrating from that rural part of the country because they had survived the Rosewood massacre, so he knew what was at stake.

Willis Evans Jr.
AKA Stack

When my grandfather finished with Willis Jr., people from the quarters had come out of their houses and had come up the hill to watch the spectacle. Oh, what a performance! We weren't taught about casting out demons during those times, little did I know, that the action that was taken was a demonstration of the holy spirit executing both judgment and wisdom. I really believed it came by the laying on of hands in a most unique way. This of course was done with the aid of his belt. My grandfather was a fair man, but he believed in spare the rod, spoil the child.

## CHARLIE REED

Family was always important to Granddaddy and he never limited his definition of family to the traditional sense. If he brought you into the fold, then your DNA didn't stop you from being a part of his bloodline. Charlie Reed entered our life in the 50s. He came to our town as part of a traveling circus. He never knew who his parents were, of course, he did mention on several occasions, that he had an uncle he lived with in Philadelphia, Penn. When he was a little boy.

He became a part of our family, and family always looks out for one another. I remember there was this one incident in which Jr. Price, Mr. Jessie's nephew, who was living with us at the time got drunk, went down in the white section of Englewood and cursed out a white woman. Well you can imagine how well that went over in Florida in an almost all white community in the 50s.

Charlie Reed

That same night a group of men burned a cross in front our yard. They sent the KKK message of anger and hate loud and clear to us. It didn't matter to them that in that house was my baby who was barely 1 year old. It shook us all. Charlie Reed along with the other men of the house spent the next night sleeping in the cars and in a nearby ditch with shotguns waiting for a return.

Fortunately, they did not return. Granddaddy reported the incident to the Sheriff the next day. He held a great deal of respect amongst the white community and he was fearless. This could have turned out much worse but because of who he was there were no more problems and no more burning crosses in our front yard.

**The Three Trees**

Our house had a unique location. Near the front left of the house, there stood a big Chinaberry tree at the right side of the house, there was a Bamboo Patch and further, toward the center, much farther back of the house stood a Cedar tree. There are a lot of things you don't give too much thought too when you are a child but now as an adult, I wonder at the significance of the house being flanked by those three different types of trees.

In doing some research I discovered that:

- **The Chinaberry tree** is believed to be symbolic of the Tree of Knowledge of Good and Evil **in** the Garden of Eden. It is also believed to **symbolize** hope and strength **in** some cultures.

- The bamboo plant is supposed to be luck and carries a special balance of Feng Shui, attracts good fortune and wellbeing to its environment.

- The **CEDAR TREE**. As with **other** conifers, due to their shape that points to the sky (heaven), cedar trees are often used as a symbol of immortality and elevation. They are sometimes associated with Mary (the Assumption of the Virgin Mary into Heaven).

The type of man he was and the type of life he led, it was no wonder that we lived in a house that was surrounded by signs and wonders. We had one tree that was symbolic of the tree of life, we had another tree that was symbolic of knowledge, and there was a third batch of trees that was symbolic some would say luck, but I would call it wonders. He did live to be a hundred. One of his favorite hymns was *"Lord I'm running trying to make a 100. 99 and a 1/2 won't do.* He was prophetic. He possessed great knowledge and he imparted much of that knowledge to me.

He taught me well. He taught me spiritual things and natural things. Things I still practice and walk in this day. He taught me about the importance of healthy eating and keeping one's system cleaned out. He taught me about why balancing your sugar was so important. His words not only had meaning but they had power. He would say to us, *"I don't plan to have diabetes"*; so, he knew what to eat to normalize the sugar in his blood to keep the levels where they needed to be. He never had any serious heart trouble. No heart diagnoses or heart abnormalities, to my knowledge.

He also would say, *"the devil would not take his mind".* He suffered a slight stroke around 85 years old and he fully recovered. So much so that when he was interviewed by the local paper on his 100th birthday he was able to speak with the reporter (the Press) for 45 minutes, nonstop, and he told things that happened at the turn of the century as if it were yesterday. The legacy of the old soldier! Sharing his story in his own words.

PRESS AND STANDARD, THUR., AUG. 23, 1984

## Rev. Evans Celebrates 100th Birthday

On Wednesday August 22 the Rev. Wallace Evans celebrated his 100th birthday. And on Saturday August 25 more than 100 relatives and friends are expected to attend his birthday celebration at Catholic Hill Church near Ritter.

Evans was born in 1884 in Orangeburg County, the son of Brantley and Lucy Evans. He left Orangeburg County when he was 21 to go to Florida because "there was good work there in them times. If you couldn't do in Florida, you couldn't work no where."

For the next 28 years he worked in turpentine in Florida and then moved on to open a lumber business, cutting and hauling cross-ties and lumber in his own truck. And he is very proud of the fact that he always worked for himself. There's always work to be found, he said, but people nowadays are just too lazy to work.

Evans was married for 53 years to Hattie Brown Evans and they had one son, Willis, who was born while they were living in Florida. Mrs. Evans died in 1960, and Evans said that he after her death he "never worried about marrying no more."

The secret to his longevity, Evans said, is being a Christian. A pastor since the 1930's, he has preached for a number of denominations including Baptist, Church of God and Holiness Churches. And living for Christ and serving God has made his 100 years happy. And, God willing, he is looking forward to 101.

Observes 100th Birthday

*The Rev. Wallace Evans with his son, Willis Evans (center) and his wife, Bertha, and their son, Gary. Gary is holding a card of congratulations to Rev. Evans from President Ronald Reagan. Rev. Evans said that he was proud of the card, even though he is a Democrat.*

Courtesy of Press and Standard archives (1984)

When I look back over his life, I realize those trees were symbolic of him and his journey. For example, the third group of trees, was that of the bamboo trees. The tree that symbolizes good luck. Ironically Granddaddy's nickname was Bless. I can remember when his family would come through to visit, one of his nephews would refer to him by the nickname his family had given him, which was "Uncle Bless".

## My Grandfather Had Crazy Faith:

Two things I remember about his faith:

No. 1 He said the devil was not going to take his mind and the devil was not going to take his driver's license.

The test and the testimony:

Now to tell the truth, he was a risky driver. He drove his truck and car with violations. His truck many times, needed serious repairs.

The brakes were not working properly. When driving to stop or slow down, he had to put the truck in second gear to activate a slowdown and to come to a complete stop.

Another time he drove the truck with only one headlight beam. He received again, serious warnings from law enforcement. He even received an insurance cancellation on another occasion. In addition, this resulted in his driver's license suspension. He fought back. Disregarding his shortcomings and numerous violations, he said it was the devil fighting him. "CRAZY FAITH" When he lost his driving privilege, he took the driver's test and even the policemen helped him to pass the written test. They asked him the question in another way, and he answered, and they gave him the credit for that and gave him back his license and as a result his insurance was restored.

The second time around, upon remembering one night he was on his way to Fort Myers, which was 50 miles away from Englewood for a special church meeting. Driving a little over the speed limit, he just barely missed hitting a state trooper which was standing right on the edge of Highway 41. With his feet mostly in the grass a small portion of his shoes on the grass and a small portion of his shoes on the highway, just yelling and waving his hand with a flashlight in his hand, saying "stop, stop". Granddaddy, momentarily, didn't break his speed, drove right on past him.

I suddenly said, "Daddy, Daddy the troopers are waving you down, stop!" He broke his speed, slowed down and stopped. One of the troopers rushed to the car and commanded him to get out. He started speaking very loudly, "why didn't you stop when I told you to stop? You didn't see me standing on the side of the road? You could have hit me, since you can't see. What if you would have hit me, since you weren't looking?"

My grandfather said, "no I didn't see you while driving, I was looking straight down the road not at the grass and off the side of the road."

Then the state trooper insisted he give them his driver's license. He refused to do so. Instead, he said this is the devil trying to stop me from getting to my church meeting. "I will not give you my license."

They finally let him go. Releasing him to go on to his Church Service. This incident took place about five miles from Fort Myers. This night, I was the one, seemingly, the most upset. Where did my grandfather get the nerves to challenge the Law Enforcement Officers the way he did that night?

This is just another example of what I call, CRAZY FAITH! Almost to run over the shoes of this man, but wouldn't take the blame? Instead, said the devil was trying to stop him. Was this unmerited favor? Was it the amazing Grace and reckless faith? Oh well, the old soldier had the victory; or really, was it because he was looking straight down the road?

Around the age of 95, he was still renewing his driver's license as a souvenir.

The devil didn't take his mind, nor his driver's license.

## Things My Grandfather Taught Me:

Who I am today is largely birthed out of my grandfather's teachings. There was no greater mentor. Teachings:

1. 1Don't look down on anybody unless you are looking down to pick them up.
2. Do unto others as you would have them do unto you.
3. When one does you wrong, don't let your heart be troubled – LEAVE THEM IN THE HANDS OF GOD
4. Your name is all you got. Don't let your name go down!

## Mission Work Outside of the Family

I was looking forward to continuing my education even though it meant I would travel a distance to attend high school. I had finished the sixth grade. This ended school life at Baker's

Academy in Punta Gorda. Granddaddy was driving us from Englewood to Punta Gorda to get the school bus to Fort Myers.

He not only used his car for school bus service but for church service as well. I remembered our second trip to St. Petersburg to attend the General Assembly. This time we were able to go to St. Pete by way of going over the Sunshine Skyway Bridge. On September 6, 1954 the 4-mile-long bridge was opened carrying two lanes of 1-275/US 19 traffic over the Tampa Bay, between Bradenton and St. Petersburg, in west central Florida. It cost $22 million and had a height clearance of 150'.

To me, it was frightening to travel over that bridge. But granddaddy with his steady hand of driving, found it exciting to have had the experience of doing so.

**Life Continuing in the Fifties**

In the late fifties, I was on the cusp of completing high school. My grandmother was in the last stages of her life and she was very concerned about me being alone after she passed. I thought she was making a deathbed wish. I remembered so well that night, I was by her bedside in Arcadia, FL. After she had suffered another stroke, she said, "Marlene, I think you should get married. I worry more about you in the event something happens."

I know how strange that this may sound in this-day-and-age, but I grew up in a time where the fundamental belief was if a woman had a husband, she would always have someone to take care of her. My grandfather had been a good provider for my grandmother, and she wanted me to have the same thing. I was married in 1956 to Mr. Joseph Williams and my grandfather performed the ceremony. My grandmother lived long enough to not only see me married but to even see her first great grandchild, my daughter Thereah.

Moreover, I remember praying for her that night, nevertheless. I asked God to spare her. Let her live to go back into the church and testify of his goodness. Little did I know that she would live another four years. This was in 1956. She was not only able to go back into the church and testify of his miraculous power, but she was able to help take care of my baby for three years.

Then there was more to remember. It is funny the *things you* hold onto I still even have a copy of my marriage certificate with the old man's signature He had beautiful penmanship.

Although I dropped out of school to care for her and lost two years of my education, it was worth it for me. I chose being a nurse for her or just being there for her rather than having or thinking of having help from others. During this period, I also helped my grandfather with the chores which included helping him with the church work assisting him by driving from one location to another, while he pastured. This really kept his hands full. He was now taken from the Murdock mission and assigned to a church in Tallevast, Fl., driving him back and forth had become much bigger role in my life. In 1959 my grandmother would remain sick off and on for the entire year.

# CHAPTER FOUR

# LIFE IN THE 60S

## Life in the 60s

The changes in our life in the decade of the sixties were like no other times. Well, my grandmother had been sick off-and-on for the last two years. In February, as a matter of fact, the last Friday of the month, Grandmother, Hattie died. My grandfather sensed that her time was drawing near. I began to see him surrender her.

They had been together for over 50 years. We got through this moment. He was still pasturing in Murdock. But having to have her funeral in the largest Pentecostal church in Punta Gorda, being such a well-known person of the cloth, people from everywhere had come to witness to the home going.

This was the only time I ever remembered not knowing who all attended the funeral. Of course, I knew there were people from Tampa, St Petersburg, Sarasota, Venice, Bradenton, Palmetto, Acadia, Fort Myers, Englewood, Murdock, North Florida, and Port Saint Joe. I am sure I have missed some more of the townships.

Yes, I really was playing a bigger role in his life. I became the official driver taking him from one place to another. He kept busy with the work of the Lord. He was now taken from the Murdock mission and assigned to a church in Tallevast, Fla. Driving him back and forth had really become a much bigger role in my life.

The 60s

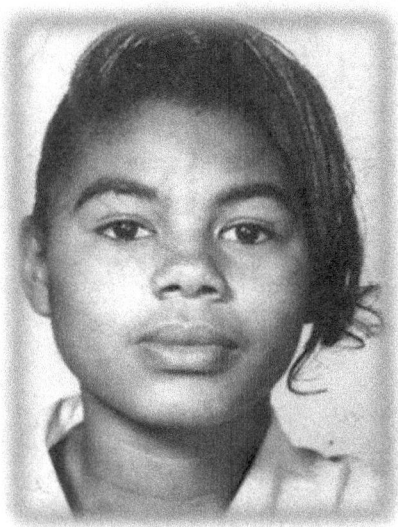

*Loreine*                              *Marlene*

1961 was the year Loreine and I graduated from high school. I remembered my grandfather telling me he would not be able to help me to go to college. However, he would help Loreine to go to college as much as possible. I had gotten married before finishing school. Maybe he felt more obligated to help her than me.

I took a full-time job working for approximately a year. Saved my money and headed for New York to enroll in school to further my education. Willis, our father had already left for New York. He had been living in Brooklyn for almost six months. I moved in with him for a short time and then got my own apartment in January 1964. I travelled back and forth to Englewood to check on my grandfather. It had become too much to leave him alone in Englewood. February of 1965, he moved in with me. He had come to New York in 1964 but he lived with his son then later, moved in with me.

1965. The year I met Mr. Melvin Askew while working for Willis Evans, my father who was managing a Mobile Gas station. I was bookkeeper. Mr. Askew was a delivery person for A. Margolis, an auto parts company. Mr. Evans was also head mechanic at the Mobile Service station. I placed many orders for parts. Mr. Askew and I grew closer together. Our relationship led to marriage.

My grandfather played such an important role in my life at this time. He traveled with me from New York to Florida assisting me in getting my divorce from my first husband. As a matter of fact, he performed my first marriage. He knew the short cuts for me. He was even able to connect me to a lawyer he knew who would be instrumental in process the paperwork for my divorce.

We travelled to Punta Gorda, Florida in the early summer of 1966. In the early spring of 1967, my divorce was final. Currently my grandfather was living with me full time. He continued to provide advice for me in our plans to marry. I was married to Mr. Askew on June 18th, 1967. Father's Day fell on this Sunday. We planned our getaway in September, the week of Labor Day into the next week of September My grandfather, of course, was with me on the trip. He was again so instrumental in instructing us as to how to travel. We drove down from New York and visited various places we visited in Florida. One of the places we went to was Fernandina Beach, where his nephew lived and owned a great portion of the beach area. We travelled from the far north end of Fla. to the almost end of the south end. Then again, cross country to Punta Gorda and Englewood, of course, this is where I grew up. I don't know who experienced the most enjoyment of the trip, my grandfather or us.

## **1968**

This year really began the greater changes in our country, both Dr. MLK and Robert Kennedy were assassinated, the war in Vietnam was still on going. Although, NY would become his main residence for the next ten years, my grandfather sometimes spent time with his son. But now, at this time, he had moved in with me permanently.

From the time he left Englewood, Fla., he would always travel back and forth to the hometown area. Indeed, he never lost his desire to travel. I remember so well, the next year when it came time to go back to Fla., he decided, I am traveling alone, I will fly. I was so troubled and afraid for him traveling alone and flying also. I kept trying to persuade him not to do so. But he in his courageous and strong spirited self, said to me, "I am not afraid. I believe in God and trust in him. If it's my time to go, then so be. My faith is in Him". I took a step back and saw myself.

I had never been on a plane and wasn't thinking about it. What a lesson I learned from the old man.

Many things came into being. Yolanda was born September 11, 1968. The next year Melvin Jr. was born, October 16th and in 1970 Patrick was born, December 20th. My grandfather was with me through it all. Praying for me and assisting me in church work as well. I rededicated my life to the Lord, becoming Spirit filled on September 30th, 1967. Yes, having my grandfather in the home served a great purpose. He was there to pray for me and minister as well. Having prayer in the home and being mentored by him, what a blessing!

When I attended church, he would be with me most of the time. Many people knew him. Many doors opened for him to preach. I remembered once he preached over the radio for a church, we attended in Brooklyn, NY. This church, Liberty Temple, Church of God in Church. A young pastor was presiding at the time. There were other young pastors opening their doors to him.

Young pastors admired him. Again, another church we were attending in which I was a member of, Pilgrim Baptist Church, which was located on Broadway and Gates Ave. It was one of the larger churches in this area. One Sunday morning, I was bringing him down the aisle to try and seat him as near the front as possible The Bishop was ministering and seeing me attempting to bring my grandfather near the front. While ministering, the Bishop stopped during his message and instructed me to bring my grandfather to him. He then gave the mic to my grandfather and requested that he pray for him.

When they saw this, the ministers from the pulpit came down to the altar area to be a part of the ones as well to be prayed for by my grandfather. What a move of God in this Sunday morning service. I remembered some of the words my grandfather said. He asked the Lord to bless the Bishop with a long life. Well, so it was. So many churches have been birthed from this bishop's ministry. He passed on June 2nd, 2018, and left behind an amazing legacy.

*Archbishop Roy E. Brown*

# CHAPTER FIVE

# LIFE IN THE 70S

I had begun to travel back and forth to attend church services in Queens, New York.

There was a situation that took place in the home. This Friday night, I had attended a service in Queens and left my grandfather at home. While in the service, a phone call came to the church, requesting me to rush back to Brooklyn because my grandfather has fallen gravely ill. After his bout with the strange illness, my grandfather decided to be baptized in the name of the Lord Jesus.

One of the things my grandfather taught me through this experience was:

## The blessing of obedience

Isa. 1:19

If ye be willing and obedient, ye shall eat the good of the land. Some would think it was a strange thing to receive a directive to be baptized (again) in the name of Jesus Christ, after pastoring or leading a flock of people for a half-century. However; God's ways are not always our ways. All he knew was that he had received a directive to be baptized and he obeyed.

In 1973, at the age of 89 years old he said to me "Marlene, would you make arrangement for me to be baptized. I immediately made the arrangements. Seeing him in the condition that he was in from that strange sickness. He couldn't even put a spoon of food in his mouth, He had lost so much of his mobility. But I took note to his obedience in being directed to be baptized and as a result, I believe that God added another eleven years to his life.

He was able to walk again and use his hands again. It was a miracle. He was restored. The written word, the spoken word, and now the manifested word were signs that were important parts of my grandfather's life.

Being obedient to his word; being healed is the goodness of the Lord in the land of the living. He lived to be 100 years old and was the fulfillment of his song. His favorite song. "Lord, I am running to make 100, 99 and a half won't do" And, therefore, the word became flesh.

While on the subject of a favorite song, another favorite song was, "Children, By and By When the Morning Come, we will understand it better By and By." Fast forwarding, I have been blessed. I have understood things much better about his life and the things I have experienced as time went by in my life.

As Time Moved On:

*Rev. Wallace Evans, 86 1970, Brooklyn, NY*

I remember, moving from Brooklyn to Queens. My grandfather was still living with me most of the time. From 1975 through 1979, we spent those four years living over a bar. Church life was about the same. We traveled back and forth from Brooklyn to St. Albans, Queens attending church services.

# CHAPTER SIX

# LIFE IN THE 80S

The eighties would be the period when we would start to see several of the old warriors pass on to glory. The assistant pastor of the established work died the summer of 1980. I flew from Queens, New York and the other family members drove from Walterboro S.C. to Fort Myers, Fl to attend the funeral of Rev. A. B. Nightingale. Rev. Nightingale was the assistant pastor under my grandfather's ministry; who later became pastor of the work.

My grandfather was already in Miami spending some time with Loreine. I remembered my grandfather singing his favorite song at his beloved friend's funeral, "On a hill far away stood and old rugged cross." It is August his 97th birthday, which was coming up Aug. 22nd.

*Rev. Abraham Nightingale*

Photo Courtesy of Down the Street by Sonja Thomas Wright

The first of the eighties was flying by. Granddaddy was at this time, very settled back in Walterboro, SC living with his son and wife. He had begun to not be able to attend church services on Sundays. He became contented in staying right home, just listening to his radio for church services and religious inspiration. He prayed and preached right in his room. You could hear him almost every morning between five or six doing a prayer or a sermon.

Things began to continue to slow down even more for him. Getting from his bedroom to the bathroom had become more stressful for him. The first of 1984 he had to be placed in a nursing home nearby. 1984 was his birthday year to celebrate his 100th year of life. He even received a commendation from the White House signed by President Reagan and Nancy Reagan.

The family planned his centennial celebration for him. August 22nd, 1884 was his birth date. August 1984, we celebrated the old soldier.

The plan for his centennial celebration was a strategic task. Family members, friends and acquaintances came from everywhere. His best friend, Mr. Jesse Mitchell who was considered as a son. He and his darling wife, Mrs. Lee came from Englewood, Florida.

*Mr. Jessie Mitchell- August 25ᵗʰ, 1984*

There were people from New York and various parts of South Carolina. Various parts of Florida, Tampa, Clearwater and Miami. His nephews and nieces from Orangeburg, his hometown. The program and ceremonial events lasted over half the day. August 25, 1984.

Each program participant shared in their own way. What it was like to know him and to share him in their life experiences. To listen to his grandchildren and great grands, it was starling. His only son, Willis Evans started the show.

Willis Evans, Jr. and his children. As the oldest granddaughter, I had my role to play. "Old soldiers, they don't die, they just start fading away". Loreine, Ruby and Chloe, the younger sisters, Of course, Loreine and Chloe as well as their husbands took to the stage and shared in their own way. The celebrant, our grandfather. What a day. Friends and many more relatives spoke. One of my dear friends, James Lee Frazier travelled from Brooklyn, New York to celebrate with us. The life of the one-hundred-year- old soldier!

Then here was The News Press interview which took approximately forty-five minutes. The things that he talked about! He told of things that occurred before the turn of the century (1899 –1912) and it was as if it were the day before. He had a phenomenal memory. The President of the United States, Ronald Reagan, sent a telegram. Hotel rooms were booked up. To be in Walterboro, S.C. this August day was an exciting moment.

The White House
Washington

We send our heartfelt congratulations. May your cherished memories be a happy reflection of the fullness of your life. We are proud to share this memorable occasion with you. Happy birthday and God bless you.

Nancy Reagan    Ronald Reagan

The Luncheon:

The Menu

Fruit cup, Baked Ham, Fried and Baked Chicken, Collard Greens, String Beans, Potato Salad, Macaroni and Cheese; Fresh Salad, Rice, Rolls, Gravy, Pies, Cakes, Coffee, Tea and Soda

Program:
Mistress of Ceremony-Chloe Coney Processional
Invocation, Ernest Coney Scripture, Mary Upshur
Welcome Address, Yolanda Askew Solo, Bro James Frazier
History Reading, Thereah Ivey Selection,
Greater St. James Choir Remarks, Mr. Jesse Mitchell
Solo, Mr. John Ivey Blessings of the Table Chat & Chew
Tribute in Song; Bye & Bye, Old Time Religion Old Rugged Cross
Speaker: Evang. Marlene Askew Selection, Greater St. James
　　　　Choir
Introduction: The Family Tree Benediction

**"Years may wrinkle the skin, but to give
up interest, wrinkles the soul."**

(Douglas MacArthur)

A work of faith and power. The old soldier, well, he just faded away and, in his journey, his supernatural strength sustained him.

*Thereah, Marlene, Melvin Jr., Yolanda, Natisha,
Granddaddy, Tiffany and Patrick*

*Bro. James Fraizer*

It was a day filled with celebration and remembrance. Many things he had told me when I was just a little girl and even when I had grown up. He would always say and declare that, "the devil is not going to take my mind". The old soldier had a testimony. His mind was kept, and keenly so. He was able to clearly state facts about the jobs that were available when he was younger and what work he was able to find. His reason for having gone to the state of Florida in pursuit of a better life.

## The Sun Setting:

I remember, the first time my grandfather had gone out and didn't come home on this night. We didn't know what to expect. But, finally, we got word that he had been hospitalized.

He had spent the entire night in Venice, Florida hospital. He had gone out to work the day before. The task that he was performing detailed using his power saw to cut the trees down in a private yard. When he had attempted to crank up the saw, he pulled the belt piece that generated an awkward move, as a result, the engine started, and the power of the engine cut one of the fingers nearly off and two other fingers one- third off. He underwent surgery for injuries and was released the next day. He was between 65 and 75 years of age then.

The second time he was hospitalized, was because he had begun to spit up blood and the diagnosis led to them wanting to do surgery to find out what was causing the internal bleeding. This was about 4 months after his 100th birthday celebration. He was scheduled to be taken in for surgery on November 29th, 1984, around 9 pm. The night before they began prepping for the surgery for the next morning, he was given an injection. After receiving the needle, he sort of flinched and turned his face slightly in the opposite direction and said "JESUS" that was the last word spoken. His time broke down into eternity. I echoed "Old soldier you didn't die, you just faded away. My experience in knowing my grandfather has left me with this inspiration.

## Aug. 22$^{nd}$, 1884 - 1984 Rev. Wallace Evans

When getting to the end of a person's life here on earth, we have a tradition of writing their obituary. So how would I sum up my Grandfather life? Grandaddy was with us for 100 years. He physically passed on Nov. 29, 1984. But spiritually the legacy he has left behind still lives on. Our family is four generations out and his influence is still being felt.

My grandfather was a foster parent before the label was used. He operated a homeless shelter before there was state funding. He helped many folks clean up and become sober before there was AA. He operated a work release program before there were parole officers. He was an entrepreneur in a predominantly white community at a time when black folks worked for white folks and not for themselves. Nine of his descendants are very active in Social Work and Community Development. Four of his descendants are ministers.

# CHAPTER SEVEN

# OLD SOLDIERS NEVER DIE...
# THEY JUST FADE AWAY

Old soldier you didn't die... you just faded away. Your days  were surely numbered. The word of destiny was in your mouth. "Lord I am running to make one hundred because ninety-nine and a half won't do". After making one hundred, upon divine appointment, supernaturally so, time in your experience broke down into eternity.

Now as you wait for your chance to tell your story as you use to also sing, "In the sweet by and by when the morning comes. When all the saints of God gather to tell the story of how they have overcome, we shall understand it better by and by. " Old soldier need I say...you left a testimony. You surely, earnestly contend for the faith which was once delivered unto the saints.

Old soldier you didn't really die... you just faded away. For old soldiers never die; they just fade away. And we who are left among them who saw this house in her first glory (which is a divine assignment). Now view it as a time to follow through. Your works will live on and your works will speak for you. Many of your prayers have already been answered and many more will be answered

Again, your works will follow you. And I have heard you say, "I want to go to that land where you never grow old and Sabbath has no end. And every day will be Sunday." Old soldier you can now sing forever.

Again, Old Soldier You Didn't Die—You Just Faded Away.

I still have the last ministerial brief case my grandfather carried.

*Grand Daughters, Marlene, Loreine, Chloe*

## Memories from His Great Grands.

Thereah
Williams-Ivey

One of my fondest memories from my childhood is the quality time I spent with my great grandfather Wallace Evans. My great grandfather was one of the most loving and caring men I ever met. As a child he was many things to me and my siblings. My love for the church and the Lord came from his example to his family.

Growing up I would love to accompany my grandfather to church. For me it was two-fold, see, I was not allowed to hang out with my friends on the streets of Bushwick in Brooklyn. Going to church was an outlet. We would go from church to church in the neighborhood. One of his favorite churches was Liberty Temple church of God in Christ.

I remember walking with him many nights up to Broadway to church. I made many friends at Liberty Temple. I also loved to hear him sing Zion songs and preach to himself. He did not need a crowd to worship. The word of God was so imbedded in him.

One of my favorite messages that I will remember till the day I die, comes from Haggai 2:3 *"Who is left among you that saw this house in her first glory and how do you see it now?* Yes, my great grandfather was the pillar of our family and we were privileged to grow up with him and it has truly been a blessing.

One of my aunts often talk about her nickname that my great grandfather gave her it was Sweet Thing, well in 1957 when I was born, I became his Sweet thing. It was my nickname until my baby sister Yolanda was born then she became his Sweet thing. My life was enriched from his love and teachings. He has truly left us a legacy.

## Octavia Evans aka TAYBA!

My great grandfather had a way of calling my name. He never called me Octavia or Tavi like the rest of our family members. For some strange reason, Granddaddy always called me TAYBA. I remember a time that Grandaddy gave me what would be a lifelong lesson. I was outside playing, and it was in the early 70s and I was about 10 years old.

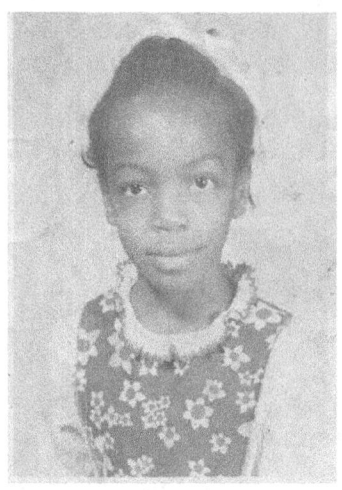

We lived in Bushwick area of Brooklyn at this time. Next door to our building was another apartment building and on the third floor a little Spanish girl lived, and she wasn't allowed outside because her mother was at work. This one day she found her mom's change jar and started throwing coins out the window to me and some of the other kids. So, we would catch the change she was throwing out the window and run to the store and buy candy. We had so much fun catching that money and spending it. It never dawned us that what later would happen, I would be accused of stealing.

Well, when the little girl's mom came home to find her change gone. The little girl knew she was in trouble, so instead of telling her mother the truth, she told her mom that we had come upstairs and stole the money. Well the mom came over to my house and told my mother that I had taken her money. I tried to explain to my mom that I hadn't stolen it but that went on deaf ears and I got the worst spanking in my life.

Granddaddy was still living with us at this point and he was an eyewitness to the laying on of the hands that day. And every time I started to get out of hand afterwards, he knew he only had to say one thing to get me back in line. He would ask me one question, *"TAYBA, I wonder what happened to that Spanish woman's money?"* And like clockwork, I would stop, get quiet or just cry. No one till this day understands how traumatic that spanking was for me especially since I know I didn't steal that money.

It is funny now, but he knew how to use his humor to keep me on track. I sure miss my granddaddy. He would laugh and laugh, and I would just sit in a corner and got quiet. I can tell you one thing no one ever had to worry about me picking up change that didn't belong to me. I don't care who threw it at me. LOL!

## Yolanda Askew

July 2004

In 2004, our family had taken a trip to Florida Yolanda Askew (great granddaughter): We had been to Florida a few times since his passing but on this trip, it had been almost 20 years after his death.

It's amazing the things you don't forget. I still remember vividly that last time I saw my great grandfather alive. He was sitting in his wheelchair outside the community center where he had just finished celebrating his 100th birthday. My uncle Stack and cousin were helping to put him back in his chair and he just kept saying, 'Oy, oy, oy".

His bones were not as limber as they had once been, but his mind was still sharp. I remember that day back in 1984 giving him a kiss and him calling me by the name he had always called me. Sweet Thing. All though my older sister and aunts claimed he used to call them that too. I still believe he knew it was me, Landa.

Sweet Thing was the name he gave the girls in the family for a period of time and when you got to whatever that magic age was, he would start referring to you by your real name. Being called sweet thing was rites of passage. I might not have been the first one he had called Sweet Thing, but I would be the last.

But I digress, in August of 2004 we would find ourselves in Florida for a family trip. This time we would find ourselves in the Fort Myers area. My Mom had wanted to connect with two of her friends from her school days Ms. Liz Perkins, and Ms. Hazel

Narrow and then my sister Tavi wanted to stop by Punta Gorda to see some other family members.

While we were on that side of town, my Mom wanted us to take a road trip down to Englewood to see if she could still find the family land. And low and behold we did. There was a new family living there but some things had not changed the bamboo tree was still in full bloom and was still there. God showed us additional favor that day because my Mom knocked on the door and explained who she was and that this was where her childhood home had been. The man who occupied the house was nice enough to let us come in and visit. They even had a floral arrangement from the bamboo branches in the house. My mom was able to bring several pieces of the bamboo tree home with us just to cherish as a special thing to have in the home.

*A Bamboo Arrangement*

Depicting the Rev. W.A. Evans Legacy July 3, 2004

But that was not the only amazing thing that day. What did we see when we walked into the house? There was an arrangement of Bamboo Tree pieces sitting on the mantel in the living room. It was like Granddaddy had phoned ahead and was saying, "Welcome Home." I can't tell you how much that day meant to my Mom. I am so glad that my sister Tavi and I got a chance to stand where the legacy began.

# THE LEGACY CONTINUES...

## EVANS FAMILY TREE

### Wallace & Hattie Evans

#### Willis Sr. Evans

**Corine**
Marlene
Evans Askew

**Mary**
Chloe Evans
Coney &
Ernest

**Bertha**
Carletha
Stephens

**Thereah** Tiffany   Natisha

**Octavia** Candice   Henry
           Syncere Capree

**Ernest Jr & Anika** Shelby
**Codrin** Antonio

**Yolanda**
**Melvin Jr. &**
**Vanessa** Justin   Jannes Jaylynn
**Patrick** Autumn   Summer

Willis Jr.
Evans aka
"Stack" &
Geraldine

Vonda Evans

**Jerome** Jerome Jr. Jamal
                     Kwamel
**Willie James** Sia
**Marie** Brittany   Ceeilla
          Tyire    Clana
**Connie** Keith    Kenny
**Darin** Yanese    Jaleah
**Travis** Cameron

Lorlene Evans
Townsel & Al

Wallace "Gary"
Evans & Kastra

**Erika** Brandon
**Marc**

Ruby Everett

Connected by blood. Connected by love.

# AND THE LEGACY CONTINUES...

My great grandfather Wallace Evans has meant a lot to our family. So much so that years later my brother Patrick and I would follow in our great grandfather's footsteps and become entrepreneurs as well and launch our own company called the Legacy Group.

***The Legacy Group*** specializes in Entrepreneurial Project Development, Program Management Services, Property Management and Acquisitions. ***The Legacy Group*** has been in existence since 2013. The co-owners of ***The Legacy Group*** are a brother and sister team that have a combined 30+ years' experience in Design & Construction, Engineering, Project Management, Marketing and Business Development.

The grand, great grand and great, great children of Rev. W.A. Evans And Your Seeds shall be blessed.
And the Legacy continues...

*Patrick Askew*
*Lecturer; Executive Vice President, New York City*
*Economic Development Corporation*

Patrick Askew is the Executive Vice President who leads the Capital Division at the New York City Economic Development Corporation. He manages a $9+ billion project portfolio, including 95+ projects in design/construction, as well as 35+ engineers, architects, landscape architects, and other technical and administrative project support staff. Patrick provides executive oversight for all capital design and construction work which includes large scale infrastructure projects, such as: construction of a water siphon between Staten Island and Brooklyn; design and construction of the Coney Island Hospital, East Midtown Greenway, and West Thames Pedestrian Bridge; he is also engaged in the development of the proposed state of the art BQX Streetcar transportation system. Prior to EDC, Patrick worked for PANYNJ overseeing design and construction of the World Trade Center site, and as a consultant for the NYCTA monitoring their $32 billion capital program.

He is a graduate of Temple and New York University and holds a bachelor's and master's in Civil Engineering, and a master's in Business Administration.

Thereah Ivey – Great Grand Daughter
Brooklyn Regional Director,
Rising Ground Children & Family
Services

Vonda Evans – Grand Daughter
Community Impact Director,
Lower Country American Heart
Association, Charleston, SC

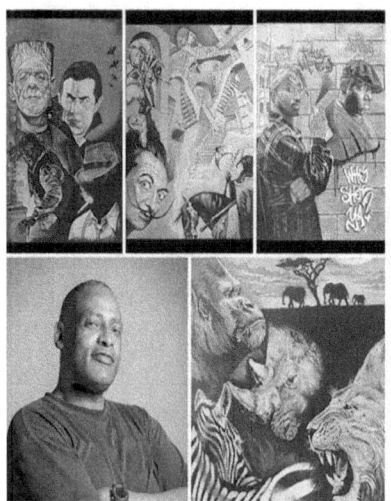 

Travis Evans – Great Grandson
Artist

Ernest Coney Jr.– Great Grandson
President and CEO, Corporation to
Develop Community of Tampa

Providence struggled last year, but post player Jaylynn Askew is helping to lead the Panther revival this season. She is the team's leading returning scorer. *Andrew Starr/MMHW photo*

# ABOUT THE AUTHOR

Marlene Ruth Evans-Askew was born January 29th, 1940 in Gainesville, Fl. She is the oldest daughter of the late Willis Evans Sr. and Corine Freeman. When she was seven months old Marlene was given to her grandparents the late Rev. W. A. Evans and Hattie Evans. She was raised in a Christian home, knowing the fear and love of God. Marlene is the first grandchild of the late Rev. Evans. Marlene's roots springs from the foundation and work of pastor and preacher, Wallace Evans, who went on to glory at the age of 100.

Evangelist
Marlene Askew

Paul was taught at the feet of Gamaliel. Marlene received her early teaching at the feet of the late Rev. Evans. Although at the time she didn't fully understand the deep calling on her life, in her youth, Marlene officiated many duties within the assemblies of the Church of God, Pillar and Ground of the Truth. She operated as the Pastor's Aid Leader and the Superintendent of the Sunday Schools. She received a unique experience by working by her grandfather's side in many facets.

With the word being challenged in her, she orchestrated his itinerary and made sure that he got from one mission to another mission. For so is the saying, He called the old because they knew the way and the young because they were strong. The beginning of this life changing experience began with the "old man".

In 1961 Marlene graduated with honors from Dunbar High School in Fort Myers Florida. With a passion to become a songwriter, she left her hometown in the sunshine state to relocate to Brooklyn, NY with the anticipation of pursuing a writing career during this period. Marlene has had one song set to music. With vast opportunities in New York at her disposal. She also enrolled in design school. Marlene has a passion for creative sewing and writing.

While still feeling the call to ministry in 1967, Marlene rededicated her life with a stronger conviction to the Lord, Marlene began to serve as a recording secretary under the leadership of Bishop Benny Shepherd of the St. John Apostolic Faith in Brooklyn, NY. Bishop Shepherd acknowledging the call on her, licensed Marlene as a missionary and appointed her as the vice president of the missionary board.

After serving faithfully at St. John in 1969, she joined under the leadership of Elder William Marbury of the Liberty Temple C.O.G.I.C. There she faithfully served in the missionary and prayer band ministries. Early in the Seventies, she was called to the evangelistic ministries. While serving under Bishop Roy E. Brown of the Pilgrim Assemblies Int'l in 1975 she was ordained and licensed through the council of churches of the New York Christian Liaison Force Inc of NYC. She also received a Bachelor of Theology from York Bible College and Theology Seminary on May 16th, 1976. Marlene begins to work faithful within the body of Christ due to the calling, she began to evangelize and mentor. She has a special calling to help churches in their infancy and to help build and restructure in the preparation of the greater works.

God had a divine purpose when placing Marlene at the side of her grandfather. Whereas God works in the mechanics of the family, many family members have come to know the Lord through her life. She now has two of her five children in ministry.

While believing God to fulfill a prophetic word to her which is not one of your children will be lost... all will be saved.

Marlene is the proud mother of five children. Thereah, Octavia, Yolanda, Melvin Jr. and Patrick. One daughter in law Vanessa. Nine Grandchildren, Tiffany, Natisha, Candice, Henry Justin, Janessa, Autumn, Jaylynn, and Summer. She also has two great grandson Syncere and Capree.

After being a stay at home mom for 12 years, nurturing, teaching and caring for her children, she re-entered the workforce in 1978 as an administrative assistant with the New York Public Library. She would later go onto working at Columbia University in the Business School. She would spend

15 ½ years working in the Graduate School of Business as an administrative assistant until she would take early retirement. Subsequently, since that time she has been blessed to tour the Holy Land, published a book of poems, launched Marlene's Creative designs all the while remaining very active in the ministry.